SOMETHING
DIFFERENT

SOMETHING DIFFERENT

STORIES IN RHYME
BY ALBERT CROSS

First published in paperback in 2017 by Sixth Element Publishing
on behalf of Albert Cross

Sixth Element Publishing
Arthur Robinson House
13-14 The Green
Billingham
Stockton on Tees
TS23 1EU
Tel: 01642 360253
www.6epublishing.net

ISBN 978-1-912218-07-3

British Library Cataloguing in Publication Data. A catalogue record for this book is available from the British Library.

Printed in Great Britain.

CONTENTS

*Dedicated to my late wife Brenda,
without whom I would not have had three wonderful children,
Stephen, Garry and Alycia, and three wonderful grandchildren,
Christopher, Alice and Matthew.*

BRENDA

You knelt down beside me that I do believe
I dare not move in case you did leave
I did not want you to go away
It was then I did realise it was your birthday
I opened my eyes but could see nothing at all
Only the portraits of my family and you on the wall
I knew you were still there in the room
I could feel the presence there
My body vibrated I shook everywhere
I was happy but scared did not know what to do
You had been gone seventeen months but I still love you

Fourteen March two thousand and five Monday five forty am

PICTURES IN THE SKY

I see faces that are happy
I see faces that are sad
I see faces that look lonely
I see faces that are mad
I see faces that are tender
I see faces full of grief
I see faces full of wisdom
And others beyond belief

I see different kinds of animals
Sheep and dogs galore
There are different kinds of monkeys
Of which I have not seen before
There are lions and horses and large white bears
There are different kinds of penguins
And birds that fly in pairs
I see the child with the smiling face
Out there way on high
But I have yet to see your smiling face
Among those pictures in the sky

OH LORD

Oh Lord above do not pity me
The time has come and I cannot see
I have a white cane but use a brown
I try to smile and not to frown
When I use my white cane
It sticks out like a sore thumb
And I am easily robbed by the guttersnipe scum
I get on with my life I have no choice
Oh Lord above please hear my voice
There are people who complain about looking at a bare wall

But would they change places and see nothing at all
I bump into the table and into the chair I crash
I am unable to bend down to pick up the trash
This is my life there is no other way
And this I will do day after day
Maybe one day I know not when
I will get some new eyes and see again
But that is wishful thinking and I do not give a mind
Because in my head I will always be blind

THE FLAME OF LIFE

The flame of life it burns for me
Through clouded skies so I can see
The tallest tree and meadows so golden
The running stream and rapids swollen
The bird and butterfly also the bee
The flame of life it burns for me

Cottages with their little thatched roofs
Horses in the field with galloping hoofs
Children in the park playing round that tree
The flame of life it burns for me

The plane that flies across the sky
With a glint of silver as it goes by
The aged and infirm and those who cannot see
Yes the flame of life really does burn for me

SIT IN MY WHEELCHAIR

As I sit in my wheelchair while I am being pushed around
I look to the heavens and not to the ground
And I think to myself what does it matter
People often stop me just for a natter

I am very grateful for their response
When I think back, I was like them once
I was very independent and walked with great speed
Now is the time when I take most heed

Some people talk through me without giving a thought
But I do not worry and I think of what I have just bought
It is not their fault, they do not understand
But I just hope one day they are not in the same band

It can be sometimes stressful but we have to press on
All the learning we do takes us back to day one

FLOWERS THAT BLOSSOM

The flowers that blossom in the early spring
Are there for the bees and the birds that sing
The flowers that blossom in August and September
Are there in the summer for you to remember

When the winter comes and the snow is deep
You look out of the window then go back to sleep
After a while you hear the birds on the wing
It is then that you know it is next spring

THE MIST ON THE HILL

The mist has settled upon the hill
It is there next morning when you wake up still
You lie back down and close your eyes
Then you wait for the sun to rise
Then once more you look at the hill again
The mist has gone and there is no rain
Up in the sky no clouds to be seen
The sheep and cows are in a field of green
The rabbits and squirrels run all around the place
They seem so tame when they look you in the face

THE WATER'S EDGE

As I walked along the water's edge
My footprints in the sand
The sea it washed over my feet
The world was in my hand
When I looked all around
I could see the distant mountains
In this lovely town and harbour
There was in the square a tiny fountain
People sat about not giving a care
Music from the little café just floated through air

ALICE

I woke up one morn
And a star was born
In the church was a shining chalice
In a cradle below sleeping soft and low
Was my beautiful granddaughter Alice

She opened her eyes and began to smile
At all the people walking down the aisle
They all smiled back and began to wave and peep
The next thing we knew she was fast asleep

HAPPY BIRTHDAY ALICE

She's all grown up now she is three
She thinks she's too big to sit on mammy's knee

She plays with Matthew her little brother
They fight over toys and throw cushions at each other

While they are fighting, she bears him no malice
So I'd just like to say, "Happy Birthday to Alice"

HAPPY BIRTHDAY MATTHEW

Now I am one and I can stand
I can knock things over with the swish of my hand

I crawl around the floor on all fours
If I can bend forward I can feel my toes

How I long to climb those stairs
But daddy's put a gate up, but then who cares

Here comes mammy with a lovely treat
Now is the time for me to eat

Daddy wants me to do something I can't handle
To climb up to the table and blow out the candle

Everybody I know is here today
Just to wish me a "Happy Birthday"
O' by the way, my name is Matthew

YOUNG AND ATTRACTIVE

She was young and very attractive
She loved her dancing and was also active

When we were married we were very naive
What people told us we did believe
We have three wonderful children and we love them all
We also have grandchildren both tall and small

One life has gone
We are left in sorrow
The next to come?
Not today but where is tomorrow

LIGHT UP IN THE SKIES

There is this light up in the skies
It shines so bright, I can see it in your eyes
Your smile is wonderful in every way
You are my night you are my day

The days go past and the months roll on
The dark days arrive and there is no sun
Winter has come and is here to stay
Through to April or even May

Then the flowers will blossom and the sun will rise
Once more I can see the light in your eyes

DOWN BY THE RIVER

Over the hill down by the river
The water it seems to flow on forever
From the beginning of time
To the end of never

Higher up I can see it gleam
Through the grass that looks so green
The most wonderful sight I have ever seen
Is down by the river
That was once a stream

THAT'S LIFE

After the thunder and lightning comes the rain
After an operation comes the pain
When your brain goes wrong and you become insane
That's life

After the rain comes the sun
You sit outside and burn like a bun
With your family daughter and son
You go abroad to enjoy yourself
With money you have saved
And what's on the shelf

You come back home full of debt
Then go to the races to have a bet
The horse you have backed must win at all cost
But it comes in last and you have lost
That's life

Money from the DHSS is not enough
You put on your coat and look like a scruff
Then you have a few drinks
And you are feeling rough
You walk in the park and over the bridge
You look over the edge and climb on to the ridge
You're almost over but for a smidge
You climb back down
That's life yes that's life

IN THE DARKNESS

I have spent hours in the darkness
Just waiting for you
To help get my clothes on
And then find my shoe
It seems such a long time
Since last you were here
The clock on the wall
Does not seem to appear
The world outside seems so far away
It is always difficult to separate
Night from the day
The summer is warm
And the winter is cold
You feel it more
When you are getting old
There are times when life is such a bind
Especially for me
Because I am blind

IRAQ IS IN TURMOIL

Iraq is in turmoil the fighting goes on
People are not happy that is nearly everyone
There is bombing and shooting every day
The politicians are trying to make peace in every way
This war will go on for a very long time
Have America and Britain created a crime
Soldiers are on duty but not by choice
They are sent out there without any voice
Wives and mothers all wait at home
Listening for good news that will make them smile
Soon their husbands and sons and daughters
Will be home in a while

NINE ELEVEN

This was the day of the 11th September
It was a day we will always remember
Two planes, they came out of the blue
Surprising everyone, not just a few
They crashed into both towers
It sounded like thunder
People looked up and began to wonder
Others were trapped by the masonry under
Brave firemen fought and some lost their lives
And those were the ones who never returned to their wives
It was a black day for all
Everyone knew that the terrorists had begun
To turn the screw
Mr Bush swore revenge, he was helped by Blair
Afghanistan was bombed daily from the air
It was then that the country was brought to its knees
People walked about and were applauding
But there is still no sign of Osama Bin Laden

GROUND ZERO

There is a place called ground zero
Where individuals go to visit their hero
There is some talk about building a new tower
But this can be stopped by people power
This must be a place for people to go
And talk to their loved ones and let their grievance show

This spot must be left as a kind of respect
With the power of God they can reconnect
Let the world see now what wars can do
We should all join together not just a few
America has been shaken to its foundations
Will they now realise that there are other nations

NIGHT IS SO DARK

Night is so dark mornings are bright
When daytime comes it shows the light
When it rains and the clouds start to rumble
Who are we that we should grumble
There is a reason for everything I know not why
Is it God and his angels just having a cry
God created this earth in six days not seven
It was on this last day he created heaven

IS THIS MY LIFE

Is this my life
What am I to do
Do I go it alone or do I look for you
Which way do I turn left or right
During the day or is it at night
Will I get a sign to tell me which way
Or do I just go on day after day
How will I know when the time has come
Will it be easy or hard like some
I know not what to expect or what will be so
I have this feeling that I do not know

AWAY FROM HOME

While away from home in the winter sun far
Away to relax
I can lay on my sunbed my brain not to tax
Music in the background is just a lovely treat
The warmth of the sun is something to cheer
Being where I am I have nothing to fear
I think of home where it is very cold
The rain coming down heavy is what I am told
I have a while to go before I leave this place
So just for now watch this space

THE MOUNTAINS

The mountains in the distance look down upon the sea
The Lord above he put them there especially for you and me
The rocks and the caves are washed by the waves
And the rain it cleans the lanes
The sun it shines for everyone
And the wind it blows across the plains

AS I SIT ON MY BED

As I sit on my bed I can hear and see
I talk to myself which is not unusual for me
I have got all my senses, I am thankful for that
I am lucky, others I know who cannot hear or see
And can barely talk, just take it from me
For those people life must go on day after day
When night time comes how many of us pray
Churches are now locked up every day
With doors that are bolted, what can we say
There were times when we could visit day and night
To walk inside was a wonderful sight
To see candles lit with a soft soft glow
And to feel the silence before we go
Now it is all gone never to return
Have we looked up to the heavens
And God do we spurn

MY BODY

My ears are for hearing
And my nose is to smell
My eyes are for seeing
With my hands I feel as well
My legs they support me
With my feet I can walk
My heart pumps my life blood
With my mouth I can talk
My liver is my filter
My kidneys keep me clean
My tummy holds the residue of which I am not too keen
Inside are my intestines which is a very large tube
And sometimes in my stomach it rumbles when I move
My head is for thinking
My brain is not so good
There are lots of things I would like to do
If only that I could

WHY DO WE MOAN

Why do we moan when things are not good
We grumble about others and not listen when we should
No one is perfect just take it from me
We all have our faults as you will agree
We live on this planet from day one
Someday we will all wake up to find
The best has all gone
Too late then to moan too late then to cry
We had our chances but let them slip by

OH FLOWER OF THE ANGEL

Oh flower of the angel you come to me
I welcome you with open arms
Oh flower of the angel you are here with me
I succumb to all your charms
I know that you are near both day and night
I can feel it in the air
It makes me feel so happy and bright
Just knowing that you are there

THE HOLOCAUST

We are on the road to nowhere
There is no sun and the fields are bare
There is no water or food to eat
There are no people for us to meet
There are no stars and the sky is black
We cannot turn round for there is no way back
There is no church for us to pray
There is no night and there is no day

THE SUMMER HAS GONE

The summer has gone and the autumn is here
The nights get long and colder I fear
It is the time of the year that the leaves begin to fall
And a little later on Jack Frost will call
People who go for a walk in the park
Are sometimes seen by cars that light up the dark
As the evening draws on and the stars in the sky
Look so bright as the moon goes by
Then the sun bright red as the dawn begins to break
People in bed beginning to wake
It is time to rise to the daily chores
With no time to listen to awful bores

LUCKY

Am I not lucky when I can see all around me
I can also hear sounds very familiar
Birds and traffic and children playing
I can talk to people and hear what they are saying
Life is such a wonderful thing
I can smell the flowers, eat the fruit and veg
Walk along the lane and touch the hedge
People go by and they give me a smile
I carry on walking mile after mile
Sometimes in the town and often in the country
I can be on my own but feel very comfy
I have nothing to fear life is so good
And I think of others who would if they could
God gave us these senses that we take for granted
There are lots of things I have always wanted
The world is being destroyed by the human kind
But we all carry on and do not give a mind
The day will come when we wake up to it all
But will it be too late for one and all
God only knows

HAVING SEEN THE GRASS

Having seen the grass so green
From the rain the day before
You never know the things that grow
Outside your own front door

Some are red and some are blue
Some are even white
They bloom so nice throughout the day
And curl up again at night

Come the frost and come the snow
They all die off forever
Come the sun and come the spring
They are back and bright as ever

A DAY TO REMEMBER

I went for a trip out yesterday
Ended in York, about fifty miles away
Went into the minster for a look around
It was there that I finished under ground

I have been inside four times before
But each time I see something more
There were Roman columns and Norman brick
Viking stone so very thick

There was this bolt with a very large nut
Set in new concrete to act as a strut
There were lots more of them placed all about
Just at the entrance and on the way out

There were things uncovered from the rich to the poor
Even today there is a running sewer
Leather and iron, even steel
Knives and spoons that looked unreal

While digging the foundations, they uncovered in their search
And came across an underground church
It could have been Christian or it could have been evil
But later they found it was Norman cathedral

I went back upstairs to visit the tower
But was told I would have to wait for a quarter of an hour
I had been there since ten thirty; it was now quarter to one
I decided my visit to the minster was done

I went outside and walked down the street
I knew then it was time for me to eat
I looked at a menu, something caught my eye
I ordered coffee with homemade steak pie

I walked round the corner to the Jorvik Viking centre
I stopped at the door, then began to enter
I have been before this is true
But each time I arrived there it's a very long queue

I went inside and sat on this seat
It went backwards, all very neat
There was fish and chicken, rabbit and hare
There was also a very large stench in the air

The air was so strong, it really was foul
Even the dog began to growl
I went up this street and into a house
The family with combs, were beginning to delouse

The state of the place almost brings you to tears
Yes, I had passed through a thousand years
I looked over a bridge and there was a boat
It was then I began to gloat

Down the steps on to my seat
I was in for one hour's treat
As I sailed down the River Ouse
What a way to chase the blues

We arrived home by coach, somewhere met
A day to remember – not to forget!

THE CAR

I took the car out for a run
It was meant to be just for fun
As I drove around the bend
I thought I had come to my end

There was this car, it was quite sporty
The driver, he was well under forty
His hands were taut, his face was white
He gave himself an awful fright

He crossed the lines that were double
He got himself into a lot of trouble
The edge was high, the bend was tight
I thought I would never see tonight

However, I managed to swerve away
Now I live to see another day

His car was damaged, his leg was broken
He gave a smile after he had awoken
The ambulance came and took him away
He will live to drive another day

As for me, the day was fraught
It left me with a little thought
When I go out I look ahead
You definitely are a long time dead!

ODD SAYINGS

Wife: I changed the bed this morning
Husband: what into an armchair

Husband: I have been for a run in the car
Wife: it must have been a very large car

Wife: I have just put the kettle on
Husband: where, on top of the wardrobe

Wife: I hopped on the bus this morning
Husband: you should walk on like other people

Husband: I have just twisted my ankle
Wife: that is what you get for cheating

THE BEACH

To see the people all arrive at the beach
Some head for the water and eventually reach
They get on their sunbeds, some have chairs
The children run riot, but then who cares?

You look out to the sea
It is so inviting
Just to go for a swim
Is very exciting

Then late on, after leaving the water
Some worried parents are looking for their daughter
But help is at hand, there is no need to cry
She has been found, playing nearby

THE DREAM

In bed one night I was having a dream
A church built in a rock in the middle of a stream
Rocks large and small with an altar so tall

On top was a portrait of a lady
I knew not at all
Someone said about dungeons below ground
I turned about but my friend was not around

Still laid in bed till about four forty five
I began to wonder if I was really alive
Beside me in bed, something was pushing
It felt like it could have been a balloon or a cushion

I was not asleep but it was a surprise
It was then I decided to open my eyes
Nothing was there to be seen in the bed
I looked around and shook my head

I laid down again not sure whether to be
Frightened or proud
Then all of a sudden, I could feel this cloud
As I looked around I could see nothing there
But I could still feel it going through my hair

THE EYE TEST

I went yesterday for an eye test
I found out which eye was the best
I looked at the chart both green and red
She told me to look up, but I looked down instead

I looked to the left and then to the right
All this to check on my eye sight
I read all the letters as small as I could
But not really as small as I should

I looked into a machine; there was a round red dot
Just like seeing into a furnace
Which was very very hot
On another machine I rested my chin
Then leaned forward and began to look in

She said, "relax, this will not hurt"
All of a sudden I was given a squirt
That was one eye, then I moved over
That was the test for glaucoma

She said my eyes were quite healthy
I think she thought I was wealthy
I sat in the chair just looking pensive
Then she brought me some glasses, which were expensive

"I cannot afford them", I said tongue in cheek
"maybe I should come back next week"
She got out another pair, then off went her bleeper
Then I finished up buying a pair much cheaper

SLEEP MY BABY

Go to sleep my baby
Close your pretty eyes
Mammy she may scold you
If she knows you are telling lies

Go to sleep my baby into wonderland
When you wake up in the morning
Mammy will hold your hand

Go to sleep my baby
Dream your dreams of course
When the sun comes up tomorrow
You can ride your rocking horse

Go to sleep my baby
Rest your little head
If mammy's not there in the morning
Daddy will be there instead

PEOPLE KNOW

People know I'm not very clever
I sometimes alter with the change in the weather
I am often quite happy but sometime dull
And I dash around like the proverbial bull

Outside I am happy – inside a little sad
I try to be good – but never bad
I help when I can for others about
And often when I talk I begin to shout

This may sound funny but I have no choice
Without knowing, I raise my voice
I write all this as I sit at home
It is known as – anxiety syndrome!

I GOT UP THIS MORNING

I got up this morning at quarter to eight
Jobs to do that could not wait
Clothes in the washer, clean the floor
Threw out a towel that was worn and tore

Did some ironing, emptied the bin
The place started to look like a new pin
I polished around, had a cup of tea
Then the postman came with a letter for me

It looked very private, it made me feel ill
But I knew for a fact it was not a bill
I opened it up and looked inside
I took out the contents and put it to one side

I left it there for a while or so
But could not decide to read it though
At last I did and to my surprise
Tears started to appear in my eyes

A cheque inside, a tidy sum
From a competition I had won
I thought what to do for the rest of the day
Then I cashed it all for a good holiday

I HAVE A PAIN

I have a pain in my leg
And a pain in my chest
Now is the time
When I should take a rest

I am quite busy
Working every day
But I like what I do
Without any pay

I help other people
Who cannot properly see
And this gives a lot
Of satisfaction to me

They come to the centre
To socialise and
Meet other people
Who become their eyes

They have tea or coffee
And stay for lunch
Bingo they play
Such a happy bunch

At two o' clock
Without any fuss
They all line up
And get on the bus

AS I SIT ON THE SAND

As I sit on the sand
And look at the sea
A lot of people there
Not only me

Some on sunbeds
And others on chairs
Some in families
Others in pairs

Kids playing in the water
Some in the sand
The music nearby
Is the local band

They put on displays
For people to see
Everyone enjoys it
Including me

I drink my coffee
And the paper I read
Some things are of interest
Others not so

I fold up my paper
And off I go!

THE SKY IS FULL

The sky is full and very cloudy
The traffic outside is also rowdy
The cars and vans go up and down
On their way down to the town
The roads are full, the weather is bad
And to see the people looking so sad

One day the sun will shine
And everything will be just fine
The people will then have smiles on their faces
As they go to different places

HOSPITAL

I went to the hospital today
For to partake in an x-ray
The idea of the plan
Was for me to have a scan

The doctor said I might have a stone
But not to worry I was not alone
People have them every day
But quite often have them taken away

I do not think there is anything there
But it can give you quite a scare
I'll go now and think ahead
Perhaps tonight when I go to bed
I will wake up twice or even more
Goodness knows whatever for

THE MORNING IS BRIGHT

The morning is bright, the sky is clear
The air is cool, the radio I hear
The news is not good, I fear to say
So I think I will go out for the day

A day in the country will do me just fine
I will make some sarnies, but not drink the wine
Ginger beer is just as good, nice and refreshing
When walking in the wood

It's nice and quiet as I walk along
The exercise makes me feel quite strong
Now as I walk along on my own
It's time for me to make my way home

MIDDLE OF THE NIGHT

I woke up in the middle of the night
It was so early it was not even light
My tummy rumbles and makes a funny noise
I wonder if it's the same for girls as it is for boys

Then I sat up to have a drink
And that set me off and I started to think
I looked at the clock it was 2.44
I looked again, it was the same as before

I drank some orange to clear my throat
It actually felt like a bottom of a boat
I thought I would lay down again for the night
But 'oh no' I picked up my pen and started to write

I looked again it was 3.02
Goodness knows I did not know what to do
I looked out the window, it was still quite dark
Then this dog in the distance started to bark

I thought I would never go back to sleep
Then this car alarm started to bleep
It kept going for a few minutes or more
The next time I knew it was twenty past four

I knew I was tired because I was yawning
Only then did I realise it was next morning

WRITE A POEM

I was going to write a poem today
Trouble is I do not know what to say
The words normally come straight out of my head
Just so they can be easily read

My head is not clear
I cannot think at all
The funny thing is
Why I bother to write at all

AS THE CANDLES GLOW

As the candles glow and begin to flicker
The prostitutes sit and drink their liqueur
Some have bottles and some have draught
Believe me they are not so daft

As the night goes by they argue and bicker
You can have your choice for half a nicker
A short time, or a one night stand
These girls are capable of taking on all the band

The morning comes, you go to bed
I think that is all there is to be said

TODAY I AM GOING TO THE SHOPS

Today I am going to the shops
Perhaps I will buy some chops
Washing powder or even soap
Buying maybe a new wardrobe – some hope!

I wander around in the arcade
I try not to be afraid
It gets so crowded as I walk around
People dashing home, I'll be bound

Going for buses, taxis too
Some even have to stand in a queue
But for me I prefer to walk
That way I meet folk and talk
I have a chat and get on my way
And say I will see them another day

I get home and have some dinner
Switch on the telly but do not back a winner
Have a bath and sit about
Waiting for my time to go out

I will go to the club and have a drink
Play some cards and win, I think
We will talk about all and sundry
Then arrange to meet next Sunday

We say goodnight
Enough is said
We make our way back home to bed

BOWLS IN DUMFRIES

I came up this weekend to play bowls in Dumfries
I enjoyed it so much I did not want it to cease

Our opponents they won but I did not mind
A great set of lads both generous and kind
The lads had a drink including me
Then we all sat down and were provided with tea

We went to our hotel got washed and changed
Then back to the club where entertainment
Was arranged
We played bingo and danced and
We even had a raffle
But much later in the night the conversation turned to waffle

Our lads did us proud when they got up to sing
Their talent surprised me as they did their own thing
I wish you Scots folk a lot of good cheer
And hope to see you all again next year

MAN IN THE STREET

Spare a thought for the man in the street
There he stands with no shoes on his feet
He has no socks and his feet are bare
People walk past and do not give a care

As he hobbles along his steps are restricted
Some people might think that this is self-inflicted
As time goes by all is in vain
The blisters on his feet show in his face of pain

Will someone help in his hour of need
And take care of this man
And give him God's speed

NO SUN

What would we do if there was no sun
All would be dark and there would be no fun

What would we do if there was no moon
The days would be short and the nights would come soon

What would we do if there were no stars at night
All would be wrong and nothing would be right

People would say that the world is at an end
But I would give all this up just for you
My friend

WISH YOU WERE HERE

Winter has gone and the springtime is here
The flowers in the gardens
And I wish you were here
The planes in the sky
And the boats on the sea
And this gives a wonderful feeling to me
Up on the moors there is a gentle breeze
Just walking along and feeling the ease
The blue of the sky so nice and clear
On top of all that
I still wish you were here

THIS WORLD

This world is such a beautiful place
Just to know its glory and wonderful grace
The green of the jungle
And the blue of the sky
Then there is the evil and I ask myself why

Animals only kill to survive and get by
But humans kill for I know not why
Some people go for fame and power
While others are dying by the hour
Surely in the name of God this should not be
I only hope this does not happen to me

THE ROAD TO ETERNITY

Every road has a beginning
Every road has an end
Most roads they are sometimes straight
And some of them do bend
But there is one road that starts in life
And it affects both you and me
And this road it is called
The road to eternity
We join this road when we are born
Be it night or be it morn
There are lots of pitfalls along this road
Mountains to climb and carry our load
We move along from day to day
We think that life is free
But time will come
When we will have to pay
And that time will be
On the very last day

MY PLACE

The wallpaper it is patterned
And the ceiling it is white
The floor it is carpeted
With a style that is just right

There is a TV in the corner
And a couch by the door
And a table lamp beside the window
Who could ask for anything more

Upstairs are the bedrooms
Of them there are three
Two of them are empty
But the front one is for me

I have wardrobes and drawers
To put things away
I change my bedclothes once a week
And open a window every day

I also have a garage
In which I keep my car
I sometimes take it for a run
But do not go very far

The garden it is full of plants and flowers
And maybe just maybe
One fine day
All this could be ours

IN THIS WORLD

In this world that we live
As we take we should also give
Giving pleasure with a smile
When all are content
We can then rest a while

Helping others to get by
Even for those who know not why
Just the odd job or helping out
Anytime when you are out and about
Then when you go home
At the end of the day thank you Lord
Is all you need to say

HEAVEN IS ALL AROUND

Heaven is all around us also so is hell
Sometimes it is not easy to know how we feel
And see the differences as well
Purgatory can be awful
With aching joints and pains

When it sometimes eases away
It is like the wind blowing across the plains

It is not easy to be happy but then when we are
The feeling that it gives us
Is like swinging on a star
There are people all around us
Who feel different in every way
You can tell it in their voices
And in everything they say

It would not do to be all the same believe me I know
But then again as we go through life
What is it going to show
Everyone comes from heaven and there we will return
And while we are here on this earth to God
Please do not spurn

TRUE STORY

I was born in 1934
When the Second World War began
I was a year past four

I went to school like any other child
Well behaved but sometimes wild
We could see German aircraft
Up in the sky, but we had no fear, I know not why

The planes had a sound of just a buzz
They were very high up above all of us
We went to school every day
And we were told that we had to pray

In 1945 we were then at peace
The fighting then had begun to cease
The men and women came back home
There was no work so they had to roam

Peace in our time it was often said
But people had to queue for a loaf of bread
Everything was rationed, even our milk
But some ladies got married in parachute silk
Things have moved on over the years
But there are still memories and the tears
People have lost loved ones and are now on their own
They get on with their lives and they do not moan
They get a small pension and have to get by
They deserve a lot more from this government
Oh why, oh why, oh why

THE WALLS

The walls in my hotel are very thin
The people next door I can hear within
I sometimes think I am in a crowd
Then all of a sudden the noise has diminished
I think then that the row has finished
But then the silence which is here once more
Is shattered by the slam of a door

Then all of a sudden the row begins
I sometimes wonder which one wins
They could be fighting over the kids I think
But more than likely it is all about drink
The children are crying because of the noise
I do not know whether they are girls or boys
Then the next morning brings a new day
I wonder why these people come on holiday

HOLD HANDS

If you and I went out together we could hold hands
As we walked through the heather
The loch with its water so still and serene
And the flowers on the hilltops with its grass so green
The buildings in the city look far away but they are still in reach every day

PLAYING BOWLS

Playing bowls is a game to enjoy
It doesn't matter whether girl or boy
Playing on your own or in a team
Who cares if you shout or scream
Sixty, seventy, eighty odd
Who said anything about age you silly old sod

When the game is over and we count the score
Sometime we are happy and sometimes we are sore
But to play in the league is so much fun
Especially if you are out in the sun

The rain does not help when playing in bad light
Especially when the opposition start to fight
The game comes to a close and we all shake hands
We pack our bags and make our plans
Some live far, some live near
Some go straight home, some, like me go to the club for a beer
We have a few drinks and we go home at night
We open the door and turn on the light

There she is with the rolling pin
We do not know whether to stay out or go in
We pray to God then
Come next week we start all over again

ONE DAY IN MY LIFE

I wake up in the morning and I begin to sing
I look at the sky and it seems like spring
The birds outside are nestling in the trees
I open up the window and feel the morning breeze
The flowers in the garden with their petals open wide
Primroses and daffodils stand side by side
Along comes the postman with a cheery smile
I am last on his round so he has walked quite a while

People go by and say hello
Some are my neighbours others I do not know
Then I go inside lots of work to be done
Washing and ironing is not always fun
Cleaned the windows had a cup of tea
Sat down for an hour and watched TV

THIS FRIEND

I have this friend who is lovely and sweet
I also know she is tidy and neat
But she smokes this horrible cigarette
I hope she does not live to regret

I tell her little stories or even a joke
But it does not stop her having a smoke
It's fine for me to talk and preach
But I wish that I could keep them out of her reach

She says she is trying to stop
If that is true then I believe her
Or is she only having a breather
The day will arrive when she comes out on top
That will be the day when she decides to stop

GOING ON HOLIDAY

I am going on holiday tomorrow
Just to get away from all the sorrow
To lie in the sun
And bathe in the sea
With a win on the lottery
This would be the place for me

Just to sit and relax
And let the world go by
With a refreshing drink
And to gaze at the sky
I will get plenty of sun
With a lovely tan
This I will keep
For as long as I can

I will have lots to eat
You can be sure of that
And after two weeks
There will be no fat
When the plane is late
And people moan
Then I will know
I am on my way home

HOLIDAY

We are going on holiday both you and I
We will do some sun bathing under the blue sky
We will go for a dip in the sea so blue and green
Such beautiful colours we have ever seen

Then go for a walk around the cliffs and bays
What a wonderful way to spend the days
Then at night we will go for a drink
With a slap up meal to fill us up I think

MY LOVE

My love is like a wonderful rose
She blossoms more the more she grows
And she wears the most fabulous clothes
My love will follow her wherever she goes

OVER THE ROCKS AND PAST THE CAVES

As I walked over the rocks and past the caves
I looked over the cliffs and watched the waves
I looked out at the sea, both green and blue
It is so beautiful it reminds me of you

Down by the coves and over the sand
Where we could walk hand in hand
But you are there and I am here
And to say that I miss you, I really do my dear

As I walk along the path
I think to myself and begin to laugh
I reach the road and I know quite well
This is the way back to my hotel

CHRISTMAS DAY IN THE BLIND CENTRE

It was Christmas Day in the blind centre
Albert had a sleep in
When he went in for breakfast
It was already in the bin

He went into the kitchen
To get himself a plate
When he came back again
The dog was there, too late

It was Christmas Day in the blind centre
Albert went for a walk
There was no one around
For him to have a talk

It was Christmas Day in the blind centre
Albert was all alone
It was so very quiet
Not a tinkle from the phone

Albert's head was pounding
It was so very sore
Because he had too much to drink
The very night before

MY DEAR

I write this to you my dear
I hope you can lend me your ear
For I want you to understand
That you will always be at hand

Sometimes I may need your advice
The answers you give will be so nice
I know they will cheer me up this way
Sometimes I do not know what to say

Please stand up and take a bow
I have to go and leave you now
I think I have arrived at the end
Goodbye to you my dearest friend

THE LEAVES

The leaves are falling and the trees are bare
The mornings are misty and there is damp in the air
The days are short and the nights are long
There are no birds around to sing their song

The autumn is here you can tell by the sky
The wonderful sunsets as the days go by
The gardens that used to look so nice
Will soon by covered with snow and ice

As the days go by and the sun gets low
It will not be long when we are walking in snow
The summer has gone and we must keep warm
We put on winter clothes and shelter from the storm

The winter is long and also cold
There are lots of stories to be told
Christmas time is time for bliss
There must be better stories told than this

ROAD IN LIFE

There is this road in life
That we must follow
Sometimes it is hard
And sometimes it is hollow

But as we pass along
We have to agree
Not only for you
But also for me

The trials and tribulations
That we are about to face
Down this road to sincerity and grace

One day we will all reach there
But only God knows when
So until that time comes
God loves us all till then

ROSEBERRY TOPPING

I walked up to Roseberry Topping
The sun was lovely and bright
I stayed there till the day turned to darkness
And the moon lit up the night

I walked down the hill in the stillness
Long shadows from the sky above
I slipped on my backside a few times
I think someone gave me a shove

When I got down to the car park
My car was the only one there
I heard a rustle in the bushes
It didn't half give me a scare

I looked around a few times
To make sure all was clear
Then I got into my car
And drove off in second gear

IN THE WOOD

Things looked good as I walked through the wood
The leaves on the trees were green
The sun in the sky was bright and high
The best I have ever seen

The birds all sang as the church bells rang
And the people walked to Sunday service
I thought about going but still not knowing
If I would be altogether nervous

I went into the church where people all sat
I knelt in the pew and took off my hat
The church was not full in fact it was quite sparse
I began to wonder if it was all a farce

At the end of the mass all the people walked out
And I began to wonder what they were thinking about
Some looked happy and some looked sad
Others seemed quite healthy but some looked bad

As I walked down the road
I thought I would help if I could
Then I decided to go back in the wood

COLD AND COUGH

If you suffer with a cold and cough
You should start with a bowl of broth
A nice brisk walk upon the hills
But do not forget to take your pills

When you come down and walk the lane
It's surprising how much it eases the pain

When you get back home do not go to bed
Two whisky macs will do nicely instead

CHRISTMAS MORNING

It was Christmas morning and all the girls and boys,
Are up bright and early playing with their toys
Wrapping on the sofa, boxes on the floor,
And you can hear the children screaming galore

Most are very happy but some children they are not
All because their parents, the batteries they forgot
It is sad to see their faces with toys they cannot play
They have been put aside for the moment to play another day

FROG AND TOAD

As I walked along the road
I came upon a frog and toad
Then I walked down the lane
There I spotted a duck that was lame
I took it to the local vet
He told me it would take some time yet
Before the duck would be fit and well
But not to worry and do not dwell
Next day I came upon a farm
I thought walking through would
Do no harm
Cutting across the field there was this bull
Having just had a meal I was quite full
Running as fast as I could go
But comparing the speed of the bull
I was very slow
I managed to reach the other side
And up a tree I had to hide
It took a while before the bull went away
I closed my eyes and began to pray
I came back down feeling much ashamed
But then again I could have been maimed
I got back home feeling very tired
I have written all this down
Because it made me inspired

HOLDING HER HAND

Just holding her hand
Was a wonderful treat
She lives far off
A long way from here
And when she goes home
I will miss her I fear
She lives in Australia
It is a far off land
I have often thought about it
But have never planned
I will go there one day
To meet this lady fair
How long I stay
Could be up to her
I shall return home
To my family and friends
But this is not how the story will end
She has her family
And I have mine
Then maybe one day that will be fine

SPECIAL CARD

I picked for you this special card
For in the past things have been hard
I hope for you the future brings
All the great and wonderful things
Maybe now you should get bolder
And then to stop looking over your shoulder
Until that time do not stand still
Just make sure you have a strong will
This card was not got for the verse
But I hope good fortune falls into your purse

SWEETS AND FLOWERS

I send you sweets and flowers
I sit by the phone and wait for hours
What has happened I do not know
I cannot get through to you
To let me know
Have I done wrong what can it be
So please pick up the phone and talk to me
Is there someone else
Then I would like to know
Because then in my heart
It will hurt me so
I cannot go on any more this way
So if it is true then we will call it a day

ILLUSIONS

I used to think that we were one
But since that day it has all gone
All my illusions have been shattered
It just feels like my heart is battered
Now I must start all over once more
With someone new I have never met before
Where she is I do not know but one day
There may be a knock upon my door
She will be there I am sure
When that happens it will be good and pure
I have been disappointed a few times before
But it is only a battle and not a war
I will win in the end I am sure I will
When that time arrives it will be my greatest thrill

CHILD WAS BORN

I went to the stable where a child was born
He was laid in a manger
Wrapped in clothes that were torn
Mary his mother just knelt by his side
Joseph was stood there draped in goat's hide
It started to rain and also snow
Then the wind began to blow
Then the cattle inside started to swarm
Around the manger to keep the child warm
The door it was open as it would be
So everyone else would be able to see
There were three wise kings
Who came from afar guided to the stable
By a bright new star
They brought myrrh frankincense also gold
Each one had its own value so we were told
But there was one king who wanted him dead
So he sent out his soldiers
To find each first born male and cut off his head
But this child grew up to be man made
He became a carpenter with Joseph his aid
He preached in the temples also the hills
He preached in the fields which had just been tilled
He preached on the mountain way up high
Then lifted his hands up to the sky
And said God I am ready to die
This story has been told for ever
So let's all join our hands together

FLY A PLANE

I wish that I could fly a plane
I would travel all over the world
And back again
North south east and west
I would make note of which place
Was the best
Over mountains across the plains
Ride a horse and hold the reins
Across the desert on a four by four
That's something I have never done before
Over the sea and across the ice
Far off places that would be nice
To fly in a rocket into outer space
Then back to earth and settle
In my own little place

SPECIAL WISH

If I could wish for a special wish
It would not be one but two
The first would be health and happiness
And the second would be happy with you
You set my heart on fire
You also set me to aspire
All for the love of you
I would like to tell you face to face
What I would love to do
But I feel so afraid I do not know what to do
If only I could hold your hand
Then I would be the happiest person in the land

THINK OF YOU

If only you knew what I think of you
Would your heart still belong to me
If only you could swim across the sea
Then I know what you mean to me
The sky so vast the planes are so fast
But that does not matter to me
I love you so much just a gentle touch
And my body shakes from a to zee

THE MOST WONDERFUL GIRL

I am in love with the most wonderful girl in the world
But she is not in love with me
I still love the most wonderful girl in the world
But those things only happen to me
She does not know I even exist
And my heart it aches so much
I know she is married but I do not care
I only long for her touch
I will follow her in my dreams
No matter where
She is so beautiful in the whole wide world
One day I will tell her so
But that could be too late for me
When she finds out I will never know

THE WAY THINGS WERE

I write these words to you my dear
I hope you are feeling well
I would do anything for you my dear
Even ring the town hall bell
And when you are up and about my dear
I will take you for a walk
We will go into the local park my dear
There we can sit and talk
We can talk about the bygone days
Also reminisce
The times I took you home my dear
And got a goodnight kiss
Things have changed now
Modern times are here to stay
But that does not matter to us my dear
I will love you the same old way

MY PAST

My past is my past what has gone before
What I have done is now a closed door
My future is next I know not what to do
Maybe tomorrow will bring someone like you
I know not who you are or where you are from
But once I have met you
I will have known all along

NO MATTER

No matter how much I love you
No matter how much I care
No matter how long the time goes
I know that you are there
It's been so long since I last saw you
You mean so much to me
Are your eyes filled with sorrow
Do you still remember me
One day I will return to you
You are the light of my life
And next time we are together
We will be man and wife

PASS THIS WAY

Only once do we pass this way
And see the light of every day
In this time of love and sorrow
God has lent to us this life
For us to borrow
Be it short or be it long
While others grieve
You must be strong
God is loving and forgiving
From this day forward
You must go on living

PREMONITIONS

Premonitions I do not know
Where they come from
Or where they go
Are they false or are they true
Could this happen to both me and you
Here we are up in the air
Flying around to who knows where
Will we get to our journey's end
Or will this be our life's last spend
This I would like to tell why
But you will have to wait
Until we all die

CARS

Some cars come some cars go
Where they end up I do not know
Some go west some go east
Some are small some are large like a beast
Some are empty some are full
Some are in Manchester some are in Hull
Some are new some are old
Some are expensive so I am told
Some roads are good some are very bad
When a car breaks down it makes people mad
Wouldn't it be nice to have peace and quiet
Instead of drink drivers causing a riot

STAY

Stay with me forever stay with me for good
Because I would stay with you forever
If only that I could
You are mine for always bright as a shining star
Everything about you is just bubbly by far
If only you were with me
That would be my lament
Then the rest of my life
I would be happy and content

OLD YEAR

The old year has gone
The New Year is here
But all the troubles are still with us I fear
No clean slate to start anew
We still have our bills to pay
Both me and you
Thinking about holidays yet to come
But that will never happen to some
Count your pennies while you can
And try to keep away from the tally man
It is not easy in this day and age
To go away at a particular stage
But never mind we will all get by
I don't how but we can only try

THE PETALS

The petals on the flowers
That stem above the ground
The green of the grass
As I look all around
Branches in the trees
Start to sway in the breeze
And in the distance it is you I have found
Time and again I have looked in vain
In the sunshine and also in the rain
You are not there what can it be
Is it an illusion or is it just me
I will keep looking every which way
Until the time comes
When you will be there one day

STILLNESS OF THE NIGHT

The stillness of the night
When the moon shines across the skies
The sadness in your face
When the tears fall from your eyes
Gone now and never to return
The aching of your body
But in your heart there is still a burn
One day there will be joy
And a smile upon your face
You will meet someone
Who will fill that vacant place
No more tears no more sighs
But lots of happiness in your eyes

EVERY CLOUD

They say every cloud
Has a silver lining
But who needs a cloud
When the sun is shining
Why do we need umbrellas
When it's not raining
And why do people
Keep on complaining
Maybe the weather
Does not suit us all
But without the weather
We would have nothing at all
Maybe we should all think awhile
And greet every one
With a welcome smile

TIME OF THE YEAR

This is the time of the year
When the shoots spring through
With a burst of colours
So bright and so new
The fields and the gardens
Look wonderful and green
And the flowers and plants
Are the best I have seen
The nights are getting lighter
The mornings they are too
I am feeling wonderful
And I hope you are too
Maybe we will go walking upon the hills
Keep away from the shops
And the ringing tills
Outside the air is fresh and free
We can enjoy the sunshine
Both you and me

A STORY

To think about a story
Or even a single word
To think about a sentence
No matter how absurd
To think of other places
That you know about inside
Then think about the simple things
That fill you up with pride
Then there is the other side
Which you would not rather know
Then there are the smaller things
That you will worry how they grow
Think about almost everything
That happens every day
Then you wonder what you worried about
What else is there to say

FOR ME

What is it you do that you do for me
Am I so blind that I cannot see
Am I getting closer or at arm's length
Will you reach out to me
When I run out of strength
I am not yet drowning
But I might one day if that time comes
Will you kneel down and pray
I would like to think that it will last
But that is up to you
But at this moment you are my friend
And I hope that it will not end

STAIN UPON THIS LAND

When I am a stain upon this land
And when my brain does not work as planned
Put me in a box without any handles
Take me to the church
But do not light any candles
Burn my body but leave my soul
The ashes will then look like burnt out coal
Do as you wish but do not mourn
I have had my life from the day I was born
Do not grieve just be glad
And also remember I was just your dad

CATHOLIC BORN

When I was young I was Catholic born
I went to church every Sunday morn
Saturday was confession day
During the morning and also evening
When I grew I stopped believing
The years went by so very fast
Then in my soul I began to search
After fifty seven years
I am now back at church
Now I am happy to be back
From this life's stressful rack
I go to church every week
So contentment in my life I seek

WHY DO I THINK

Why do I think the way I do
Because what I think
I know will not come true
My head it is sometimes all of a whirl
All because of this beautiful girl
She knows nothing of this
That I am sure
She is lovely and kind tender and pure
I would love her to know
But cannot tell her so
If she knew me all would be lost
And that would be to my final cost

WHY DO WE ACCEPT

Why do we accept what goes on today
When we do not know what happened yesterday
Because when tomorrow comes
It will be another day
And today will be another yesterday
Time goes by so very fast
And things today they do not last
Before we know it we are very old
And when the winter comes we feel the cold
No going out to enjoy ourselves
We stay indoors just cleaning shelves
All we can do is be house proud
When our hearing goes we shout out loud
The telly is on but we cannot see
But we follow the soaps both you and me
And when that life goes round the bend
Then everything will be at an end

MAJORCA

With the walls so white and the roof tops red
In the evening sunshine the shadows are shed
All individual houses none are the same
Bought by people with money but who is to blame
Very large dogs and also cars
Solar heating that face to the stars
Set in lovely surroundings all nice and sublime
I do not envy them but I wish one was mine

SIT AND POSE

Would you have me to sit and pose
And paint me like a beautiful rose
Would I be pink or would I be red
Do I stand up or sit down instead
My long lovely legs they would be the stem
Others would look and be surprised at them
Would I be in a pot or stood in the ground
That would be nice with soil all around
My thorns would be sharp and my leaves would be green
I would bloom in the winter with a snowy scene
Would I be on paper or canvas in a nice wood frame
That would not matter it would just be the same
In a gallery or just in a room
But who cares about that if I am lovely in bloom

THE RIPPLING

The rippling of the water
As it weaves through the rocks
The creaking of the gates
When they open up the locks
The twittering of birds
As they nestle in the trees
The roaring of the waves
Upon the open seas
The whistling of wind
As it blows all around
The pounding of the rain
As it bounces off the ground
The mountains so high
With snow in their ridges
The majesty of the ships
As they sail beneath the bridges
The wonder of the sun
As it shines through the day
And the twinkling of the stars
So very far away
Everything is special
Across this wonderland
Then all will be as it was planned

TRANSPORTER BRIDGE

As the sun goes down
The Transporter Bridge lights up the town
From place to place everyone can see
That's everyone else including me
The Transporter Bridge is one hundred years old
But it is still standing high bright and bold
It carries people buses trucks and cars
With great steel struts and heavy bars

VIP

Yes I am a VIP but you would not think so
Just by looking at me
People walk by and do not know
But then again I cannot blame them though
To other people I look alright
It is not their fault if I am losing my sight
As I walk down the road which is difficult for me
It is easy for others as you must see
Stopping buses which I often do
They usually are the wrong ones
But what can I do
The drivers sometimes give me a glare
But I cannot read numbers
That are just a blare
Maybe one day things may change
And I will see things within my range
Oh, yes, VIP means visually impaired people

MY SOUL

You are my soul you are my life
Although you are gone you are still my wife
I think about you night and day
And I close my eyes and begin to pray
When you came back that was quite awhile
But I shall never forget that smile
I am now waiting for your return
Because in my heart there is still that burn

LIFE ONE DAY

You came into my life one day
It almost took my breath away
Before that day I knew you not
But since that day I have not forgot
You have turned my life upside down
And I even begin to act like a clown
Sometimes silly sometimes sad
I make mistakes but I am not really bad
I would like to think on a day like this
We could start off with one little kiss
Who knows this could lead to something real
Now you know just how I feel

FACE IS SO BEAUTIFUL

Your face is so beautiful
Your smile is so sweet
And when we are not together
That's the time I wish to meet
I know you are lately departed
And maybe feeling low
But life has to go on
And start as you mean to go
The present will not last forever
One day it will come to an end
So in between that time
Would you please be my friend

FACE IT IS SPARKLING

Your face it is sparkling
Your eyes they are blue
Your skin it is soft and gentle
Can this be really you
Lately you have looked tired
Drawn with lots of strain
Could this have been the virus
That gave you lots of pain
It is nice to see you happy
Full of the joys of spring
Let's hope you can be like this always
And not just in the spring

BOOK STORE

I went to the store to buy a book
When I got there all I could do was look
Some were large and some were small
There was so many books I could not read them all
Some were hard and some were soft
There were lots in the basement and some in the loft
Some were new and some were old
Some were priceless so I have been told
I opened one up and turned the page
I had to be very careful
Because of its age
As I walked down the aisle I did not know what to say
I had such a wonderful time
I am going to come back another day

NEW STAR IS BORN

Every second a new star is born
And someone on Earth begins to mourn
These stars have been there for millions of years
And people have been also shedding some tears
Their earthly bodies have now disappeared
There is only the spirits that have now and again appeared
For every spirit there is a star up in the heavens so very far
And one day they will all come down
And also Jesus wearing his crown

LYING IN BED

Here I am just lying in bed
With all sorts of things going round in my head
The weather outside so very cold and wet
Even the snow has not melted yet
The sky is so full the sun is not there
But I am cosy and warm
And I do not give a care
There are lots to be done all over the place
So I will put things away till I have time and space
The weather will change
Of that I am certain
Then in comes the sun when I pull back the curtain

LIKE TO DO

If I could do what I would like to do
Then everything would be alright
But I cannot do what I would like to do
Because I am losing my sight
When I walk down the road I just cannot find
The things I am looking for
But I do not give a mind
Things are not always easy
What others do every day
Like just going to the shops
Or going on holiday
I wake up every morning
And I am grateful for that
Then someone comes to visit me
And we have a little chat
It can be very lonely being on your own
But then again you put up with it
And try not to moan
If I could see like others can see
I would not be writing this
But then again as you can see
I will have to close like this

TINY CHURCH

In a tiny church was a beautiful altar
It looked so wonderful I could not falter
The whiteness of the tiles surrounded by gold
The statues displayed that looked so old
The tiles on the floor were old and cracked
The pews were delicate and easily moved
Money is needed for it to be improved
One lady was covered in a red silk gown
With a picture of Christ down her back
Wearing a crown

NOTHING NEW

Starting a new life is nothing new
It happens to most people both me and you
When we grow up and have a great time
And then we meet someone and all is sublime
Then we get engaged and things start to change
We start saving for the future
And a wedding we arrange
Along come the children one by one
Two might be daughters and the other a son
You will love them and they will love you
Then it will be their turn to start anew

LIFE

Life is such a wonderful thing
But it is far too short to do everything
Time goes by at a tremendous pace
We do not know if we should slow our pace
We hurry along every day
Not finding time even to pray
If only we could slow down
That little bit more
We would see things
That we missed before

DOES NOT MATTER

Lord it does not matter
Whether you are far or near
All we know is that you are here
Whether we are weak or we are strong
You will be with us all along
This road in life is not so straight
So some of us will have to wait
The Lord is waiting round the bend
And we will all get there in the end

NURSERY RHYME

Monday is the first day of the week
Monday is the first day of the week
When you get to Tuesday, Tuesday is the second day,
Tuesday is the second day of the week

Tuesday is the second day of the week
Tuesday is the second day of the week
When you get to Wednesday, Wednesday is the third day of the week
Wednesday is the third day of the week

Wednesday is the third day of the week
Wednesday is the third day of the week
When you get to Thursday, Thursday is the fourth day of the week
Thursday is the fourth day of the week

Thursday is the fourth day of the week
Thursday is the fourth day of the week
When you get to Friday, Friday is the fifth day of the week
Friday is the fifth day of the week

Friday is the fifth day of the week
Friday is the fifth day of the week
When you get to Saturday, Saturday is the sixth day of the week
Saturday is the sixth day of the week

Saturday is the sixth day of the week
Saturday is the sixth day of the week
When you get to Sunday, Sunday is the seventh day of the week
When you have been through all the days
Then it is time for your holidays

MY BRAIN

My brain is not good
I am not thinking straight
My mind is so full
But that can now wait
I will start at the beginning
On the first page
Even chapter and verse or at another stage
My heart is so heavy
Why I really do not know
Sometimes on my own
I am feeling quite low
I do not know what I really want
All the jokes and stories
Are just a big front
My life at this moment is just pending
Maybe in time there will be a happy ending

ONE HUNDRED YEARS

It is one hundred years since the First World War
Everyone said there would be no more
But in nineteen thirty nine it all began again
Germany invaded Poland which became very plain
Holland and Belgium even France
These countries just did not have a chance
It was then that Britain came into the war
And lots of people did not know what for
It became obvious after a while
Everyone had to change their living and style
We all had gas masks and even shelters
Bombs kept dropping and somewhere belters
After six long years at last it was over
But that did not mean we could all live in clover
Everything was rationed clothes and food
Standing in queues put people in a bad mood
Then came the time when people could borrow
And spend today like there was no tomorrow
But history will tell us that this one hundred years
Was only the beginning
There is another four years to nineteen eighteen
Only then will it be the end

PEOPLE ARE BORN

People are born with lots of pieces
Just like a jigsaw puzzle
But these pieces are not material
But are in the mind as we go through life
These pieces are placed in the jigsaw of life
Some may be placed in the wrong position
That is what is called a mistake
We all make mistakes in our lives
Maybe the more mistakes we make the longer we live
So the wrong piece in the jigsaw
Has to be replaced and the right one put in
And when we finally place the last piece
In the jigsaw then it will be complete
And so will our lives

NEW LIFE IS BORN

Every moment a new life is born
Not only human but animal creature and plant life
But as life is born other life dies
Is this how it is meant to be
How long has this creation been going on
And how long will it last
When did it really start and how will it finish
Did it start with a big bang like we are told
And will it finish with a big bang
Of the human kind who knows
In the past humans have made it a better place
But also made it worse
Could this be because of what we are
And what we are going to be and what of the future
Or will there be a future life is precious

REMEMBER

Remember when we played games both me and you
Snakes and ladders and Ludo too
I remember
Remember when we played I spy
You got it right and I would cry
I remember
Remember when we went to school
Other kids made me look a fool
I remember
Remember in school we had certain tasks
Then the sirens went we put on gas masks
I remember
Remember when we went to the park
We played all day till it was dark
I remember
Remember the Second World War
Get that light out
And a knock on the door
I remember
Remember when we went to the Flix
To see Roy Rodgers and Tom Mix
I remember
Remember when we sat in the back row
We misbehaved and were shown the door
I remember
Remember when we had our first kiss
We held hands and it was bliss
I remember
Remember when I got my suit and your new dress
We went to church and we both said yes
I remember
Remember when homes were to rent
Now they are called letting
And now I have a good memory for forgetting

SOME TIME AGO

Some time ago
When I went to school
We were told to sit down
When we sat down
We were told to sit up
When we all stood up
We had to stand straight
Heads held high shoulders back
And to concentrate
We went to school every day
Always early and never late
Then after school we would roller skate
Up the avenue and down again
Sometimes we would fall over now again
We picked ourselves up
Brushed ourselves down
We did not cry we did not frown
The nights were light till 11 pm
But we were in bed long before then

TALKING

I talk to you every morning on my way to town
I talk to you every evening when the light is closing down
I talk to you on the telephone I even send you texts
But when I try to talk to you face to face
You are always with your ex
I send you emails every single day
But when I want an answer you have nothing else to say
I talk to you in the sunshine also in the pouring rain
But what really gets me down is this awful bloody pain

THINKING

When I sometimes start to think
About the presence or sometimes the past
If I think about the future it does not always last
I think about the good old days
All about that and this I remember the good times
And it was really bliss
Walking to the Albert Park which was a long way off
We went into the paddling pool with our shoes and stockings off
The swings and slides were such great fun
We would forget about the time
We would get home very late

UNKNOWN

I am in a place that is unknown
No TV computers not even a phone
This is a place way out there
But it is a place I know not where
The silence is deafening I cannot explain
I am as light as a feather
And I feel no pain
There is nothing about me
That I can hear
But at the same time I have nothing to fear
There is no one around me that I can see
So when I die this is where I want to be

WORDS FROM ME

There are words I would like to say
From me to you so you can read one day
These words are difficult for me to speak
Because if I did I would blush from cheek to cheek
So I write them down all in rhyme
This is the only way and the only time
I only hope you will understand
And maybe one day hold my hand

SHOPPING

You work very hard to get your wages
You decide to go shopping that you have not done for ages
You get a bonus and expenses
So off you go to Marks and Spencer's
There are coats and trousers socks shirts
For the ladies there are tights and panties frocks and skirts
You are in the shop, people are talking
You see some boots especially for walking
There is fruit and veg frozen food too
Fresh cream cakes just for you
There are wines and spirits and all kinds of beer
For wishing your friends very good cheer
When you have spent most of your money
And all of your expenses
Now is the time to leave Marks and Spencer's

SCOTTISH ROOTS

Your Scottish roots are marvellous
You are beautiful and serene
I don't know where you came from
And I don't know where you've been
I love your Scottish accent
I love your Scottish smile
I love everything about you
Please stay with me awhile
You are mine forever
That I hope will be
And I hope that one day
You will say the same to me
Peas in a pod both you and I
And I will always love you
Until the day I die

31628775R00083

Printed in Poland
by Amazon Fulfillment
Poland Sp. z o.o., Wrocław